G000047379

CONTENTS

Photographers: Dr. Herbert R. Axelrod, Thomas Brosset, W. De Grahl, Michael Gilroy, R.H. Grantham, Harry V. Lacey, Courtesy of Midori Shobo, Max Mills, A.J. Mobbs, Irene and Michael Morcombe, Fritz Prenzel, Elaine Radford, L. Robinson, Courtesy of San Diego Zoo, G. Taylor, Dale Thompson, Louise Van Der Meid, Courtesy of Vogelpark Walsrode.

Overleaf: *Rainbow lories. The popularity of lories has been steadily increasing due to their colorful plumage and interesting personalities.* **Pages 94–95:** *A pair of black-capped lories.*

ACKNOWLEDGMENTS

Special thanks go to Glen Bushor of the Brookfield Zoo and Dr. Roland Whaley Winterfield of Purdue University's School of Veterinary Medicine, without whose help this book would not have been possible.

© **Copyright 1990 by T.F.H. Publications, Inc.**

Distributed in the UNITED STATES by T.F.H. Publications, Inc., One T.F.H. Plaza, Neptune City, NJ 07753; in CANADA to the Pet Trade by H & L Pet Supplies Inc., 27 Kingston Crescent, Kitchener, Ontario N2B 2T6; Rolf C. Hagen Ltd., 3225 Sartelon Street, Montreal 382 Quebec; in CANADA to the Book Trade by Macmillan of Canada (A Division of Canada Publishing Corporation), 164 Commander Boulevard, Agincourt, Ontario M1S 3C7; in ENGLAND by T.F.H. Publications Limited, Cliveden House/Priors Way/Bray, Maidenhead, Berkshire SL6 2HP, England; in AUSTRALIA AND THE SOUTH PACIFIC by T.F.H. (Australia) Pty. Ltd., Box 149, Brookvale 2100 N.S.W., Australia; in NEW ZEALAND by Ross Haines & Son, Ltd., 18 Monmouth Street, Grey Lynn, Auckland 2, New Zealand; in the PHILIPPINES by Bio-Research, 5 Lippay Street, San Lorenzo Village, Makati Rizal; in SOUTH AFRICA by Multipet Pty. Ltd., 30 Turners Avenue, Durban 4001. Published by T.F.H. Publications, Inc. Manufactured in the United States of America by T.F.H. Publications, Inc.

LORIES

MICHAEL W. GOS

The 21 subspecies of the rainbow lory exhibit extensive color variation. ***Left:*** *Mitchell's rainbow lory,* Trichoglossus haematodus mitchelli. ***Below:*** *Swainson's rainbow lory,* Trichoglossus haematodus moluccanus.

What Are Lories?

Virtually every novice in the field of aviculture sooner or later looks to the parrot family as a source for the future pet. For many of these hobbyists, beauty of appearance is a top concern. When that is the case, the subfamily Loriinae is of great interest. Some of the most beautiful birds in the world are lories, so it is understandable that the novice would take an interest in this subfamily.

Lories are often called the brush-tongued parrots because of the papillae covering a portion of the tongue. As with most evolutionary developments, the tongue is designed for the specific needs of the parrot. Lories are nectar-eaters. In the wild, they

obtain the needed food from flowering plants. They also consume juice from the various fruits and pollen they happen to pick up while searching for nectar. The papillose tongue, with its tremendous surface area, is housed in a long, narrow bill.

Lories obtain their nectar in a manner that is different from that employed by hummingbirds. It has been observed that lories crush flowers in their beaks and then suck up the juice produced. Along the way, the pollen released is packed neatly by the tongue into wads that can be easily consumed. Fruits are eaten in much the same manner. This habit of crushing flowers makes lories hard on plants and, as a result, they are seldom recommended for the planted aviary.

In the wild, lories are native to most areas of the South Pacific. Truly tropical birds, they can tolerate much heat, but being native to islands with high mountains, most lories are also cold-hardy, since temperatures drop drastically at night in the high altitude environments. They are so cold-hardy, in fact, that only one of the commonly kept species, the fairy lory, needs heat in the winter.

Most lories, particularly the common Swainson's or rainbow lory, can be found around coconut plantations in the South Seas. These gorgeous birds, which command such a high price in America and Europe, are considered pests in their native countries and are often killed by local farmers. It is a pity that they are not instead trapped and brought to countries where they are popular as pets. However, many countries, Australia in particular, ban exporting native bird species. As a result, most lories purchased in the U.S. are either from places where wildlife trade is still allowed or are bred here by aviculturists interested in increasing the popularity of the birds. The prices remain high.

Arboreal by nature, lories not only feed in trees but also spend most of their lives off the ground. They tend to be climbers rather than fliers, and this characteristic shows in the aviary where flight space is severely limited.

Smaller than the macaws or most Amazons, lories command attention because of their bright colors. Their size is also an advantage for persons who want a house pet or wish to keep lories in a limited way. Most lories are no larger than a lovebird. Nevertheless, in spite of their convenient size and beautiful appearance, lories are not often kept in the home. In fact, at this time lories in America are confined primarily to zoos. The main reason for this is a battery of problems presented by their unusual diet.

When the decision is made to take on a lory as a family member, there is much the bird can offer.

Swainson's rainbow lory in a natural setting. This bird is also known as the blue mountain rainbow lory.

Lories kept in captivity have a reputation for achieving great rapport with their owners or, in the case of zoos, their handlers. This is especially true if the handler is of the opposite sex to that of the bird. There are reports of lories liking all individuals of the opposite sex and registering moderate boredom or even contempt for persons sharing the birds' sex.

While lories generally display an even disposition, they have a certain weakness: they are not reliable. They tend to be high-strung and as a result they excite

Left:** The nominate rainbow lory species,* Trichoglossus haematodus haematodus. *This race is sometimes called the green-naped lory.* ***Below: *Red-collared rainbow lory,* Trichoglossus haematodus rubritorquis. ***Opposite:*** *Massena's rainbow lory,* Trichoglossus haematodus massena.

Purple-crowned lorikeet, Glossopsitta porphyrocephala. *Birds of this species have travel routes that follow the seasonal blossoming of gum trees.*

easily. During periods of excitement, they often have a tendency to nip.

While lories as a whole are not the best talkers, some can become quite good at imitating human speech. This is particularly true of the *Eos* and *Lorius* species.

Most lories tend to be monogamous in the wild as well as in captivity. This makes it easier to maintain a breeding system once the birds have begun. Like many other creatures, lories prefer to choose their own mates.

One major difference that separates the lories from all other psittacine birds is the ventriculus or gizzard. In all other parrots, this digestive organ is highly developed and very muscular. This enables most members of the parrot family to subsist on a diet of seeds and fruit. Lories, on the other hand, have a very weak, non-muscular ventriculus, making seed-eating impractical and possibly dangerous. Without a strong gizzard, lories have no way of digesting seeds once they are consumed.

Unfortunately, the two differences (tongue and gizzard) between lories and other parrots are not easy to see, making identification difficult. Unless the bird is feeding, the papillae on the tongue are hidden by a series of folds. The ventriculus is visible only surgically. Hobbyists who want to be able to recognize lories on sight will have to learn the appearance of the individual species and do the best they can with that knowledge. There are no easy tipoffs.

The beautiful coloration of the lories has made them more and more attractive to hobbyists who are willing to learn about the proper means for keeping these birds.

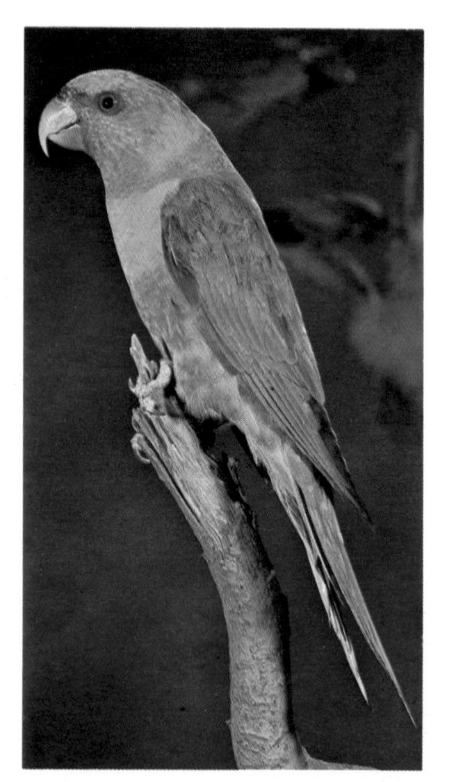

Rainbow lories are widely distributed along the Australian coast and on neighboring islands. ***Above left:*** *Weber's rainbow lory,* Trichoglossus haematodus weberi, *is found only on Flores.* ***Above right:*** *Edward's rainbow lory,* Trichoglossus haematodus capistratus, *is from Timor.* ***Opposite:*** *The blue-faced rainbow lory,* Trichoglossus haematodus intermedius, *lives in New Guinea and on Manam Island.*

The Lory Controversy

In spite of all the good points of lories, they have never been popular birds with home aviculturists. Currently, most of the lory patients seen at veterinary clinics are from zoos. Members of Purdue University's veterinary school, one of the nation's largest, never see a lory from a private home. One would suspect that this is a result of problems inherent in lories because of their diet. Over the years, lories have been the victims of a lot of bad press. Even now, most zoo keepers would tell a potential lory owner to get a seed-eater instead. As justification for that stand, the novice will probably hear the following arguments:

1. The diet of lories is too difficult for a novice to maintain. Twice a day feedings of different formulas is not something an individual will continue doing for long.
2. Because of their diet, lories' droppings are messy. As a result, the birds cannot be kept in a house.
3. Because of their temperament, they cannot be kept with other birds.
4. Since they are tropical birds, they cannot cope with cold drafts.

Essentially, proponents of the above arguments are correct to a degree. Lories are not the easiest birds to keep, but like anything else in life, you get out of it what you put into it. If you want the most beautiful parrots, it will take some extra work. The end result seems like a fair trade.

What the novice must do, then, is to decide whether or not lories are for him. A step-by-step look at the objections and their counterpoints will often clear up any confusion on the matter.

First, the diet. Granted, mixing a nectar recipe and a fruit mix is considerably more time consuming than filling a bowl with seed in the morning. However, the mixes can be made in quantities sufficient to last several days and refrigerated until needed. The ingredients can be hard to find and expensive, but there are ways for both obtaining and paying for the supplies. A careful reading of the feeding chapter will let the novice know all he is in for. The hobbyist willing to do all the things necessary to provide the healthful diet should have no problems feeding the birds; they will receive as healthy a diet as is currently available.

It is inevitable that liquid food eaters have liquid droppings. Further, lories have a tendency to "launch" their droppings a considerable distance. The droppings are considerably more odoriferous if allowed to

Opposite: *Although the keeping of lory species is somewhat more complicated than that of other parrot groups, most hobbyists think they are worth the trouble.*

Left: *Goldie's lorikeet,* Trichoglossus goldiei. ***Below left:*** *Perfect lorikeet,* Trichoglossus euteles. ***Below right:*** *Yellow-and-green lorikeet,* Trichoglossus flavoviridis meyeri. ***Opposite:*** *Johnstone's lorikeet,* Trichoglossus johnstoniae.

accumulate than those of other birds. Nevertheless, all these problems can be overcome with a little extra work on the part of the hobbyist. Launched droppings are not a problem in the outdoor aviary. Since all birds do better outdoors anyway, building a cage outside will take care of two points at once. But even if one lory is wanted as a house pet, there is still no reason why it cannot be kept neatly. Budgie owners discovered long ago how to handle their messy pets. See-through glass or plastic walls one-third of the way up the cage serve to greatly reduce thrown seed and feathers. While droppings are a little more disagreeable than either seeds or feathers, the lory is a little less messy about it. The same trick will keep all droppings within the confines of the cage quite well. It must be remembered, though, that the perches should be placed low enough so that the bird cannot discharge droppings over the glass walls. Of course, the walls will need to be cleaned

A quartet of blue-crowned lories, Vini australis. *In the wild, blue-crowned lories travel in flocks of six to 12, following the flowering of coconut palms.*

Chattering lory, Lorius garrulus flavopalliatus. *Always keep in mind that lories, like humans, have individual personalities.*

daily, and at the same time the flooring in the cage should be cleaned as well. Such daily cleaning assures that no foul smells will develop. Also, good hygiene prevents the bulk of bird diseases.

Temperamentally, all lories, just like all humans, are different. There are those that have constantly nasty dispositions when it comes to other birds, but more likely a normal-tempered bird will have periods of nastiness when something sets it off. At Brookfield Zoo, a pair of Swainson's lories lived peacefully together until one day one of them learned it could escape from the parrot cage by crawling through the hole where the now-unused seed cup once was. Whenever curator Glen Bushor would catch the marauder and put it back in the cage, the other lory would immediately attack. Just a case of jealousy? Probably; lories seem to respond to the same emotions as humans and are as unevenly tempered. Some lories can be kept in group

***Above:** A varied lorikeet,* Trichoglossus versicolor. *Members of this species frequent the tropical lowlands of northern Australia.* ***Opposite:** Ornate lory,* Trichoglossus ornatus. *Ornate lories dwell on the larger Indonesian islands.*

Purple-crowned lorikeet coming in for a landing. Since many lories experience temperature variations in the wild, most birds can withstand temperate winters if they are properly acclimated.

aviaries and others cannot. It is best not to try in any case. If the birds cannot have a run of their own, then they are probably not a wise choice.

Lories are indeed tropical birds, being native to much of the South Pacific. But anyone who has toured the South Pacific knows that the volcanic islands that dot the area are mountainous and have markedly different temperatures between sea level and mountain top. Lories in the wild often spend time in the mountains and weather this quite well. In fact, they may be able to withstand the cold better than any other member of the parrot family. Nevertheless, it is true that, like other birds, they cannot handle cold drafts. A simple shelter built at the end of the outdoor aviary will allow nearly all lories to be kept outdoors year-round without heat in all but the severest cold. This means that over most of the U.S., lories can be kept outdoors all year. The only catch is that a bird must first be placed outside during the warm months of the year so that it may acclimate gradually to the winter temperatures. In the house, a lory will do fine except in front of an open window in winter. Keeping the bird away from drafts coming through a regularly opened door will guarantee problem-free warmth.

There are problems with lories and there are ways around the problems. It cannot be overstressed that the novice must make a big and permanent decision before adding a lory to the family; a lory is not going to be easy to keep, but it can be done. If successful, the hobbyist will be keeping one of the most beautiful birds on earth. Lories are expensive to buy and can be expensive to maintain. Perhaps that is why they are seen mainly in zoos. If the decision is to go with lories, then the owner must learn all he can about the birds and be prepared to go the extra mile for their benefit. At the same time, he should anticipate being the beneficiary of the kind of pleasure that only lories can bring.

The musk lorikeet, Glossopsitta concinna, *is named for the musky odor it exudes.*

Opposite top: *A two-week-old scaly-breasted lorikeet nestling,* Trichoglossus chlorolepidotus. ***Opposite bottom:*** *A six-week-old scaly-breasted lorikeet; note how the feathering is coming in.* ***Above:*** *A scaly-breasted lorikeet with adult plumage.*

Choosing The Bird

If after reading the last two chapters the next addition to the family will still be a lory, then it is time to choose the bird and the housing. It is preferable to have the cage or aviary prepared for immediate installation of the bird upon its arrival. Both types of housing are discussed at length in the chapter on care of lories. Once the housing is set and provisions have been made for dietary needs, the hobbyist must then select the bird.

In any branch of the avian hobby, there are two sources commonly used for procurement of pet birds: pet shops and breeders.

With lories, there is often no choice in the matter. A hobbyist must take them where he can find them, if he can find them at all. Generally the question of source is academic.

Probably the biggest difference between birds bought from a pet shop and those bought from a breeder is origin. Dealers usually sell imported birds whereas breeders generally sell aviary stock. That may not be important if your bird is to be a single house pet. If, however, breeding is an objective, captive-bred birds tend to breed more easily and more successfully than do wild birds.

Whenever a lory is to be purchased, it is important that the hobbyist rely on the integrity of the source. It is better to wait months for a bird and get it from a source with a reputation for selling healthy birds than to obtain one sooner only to lose it in a matter of weeks. When a bird dies shortly after arrival in the new home, the problem can generally be traced to the source of the bird.

In the U.S., much effort goes into ensuring the health of imported birds, to a point. The result is a higher priced bird that is certified free of one disease but has possibly been exposed to many others.

When a bird first enters this country, it is placed in a quarantine station. The purpose of this quarantine is to filter out all cases of Newcastle disease, an honorable objective. However, this purpose has nothing whatsoever to do with the parrot's general health. Newcastle disease is transmissable to poultry. A strong agricultural lobby has enabled the quarantine stations to concentrate only on that disease. There is no care taken for the general health of the bird. Once the quarantine period is over and the bird is believed to be free of Newcastle, it is allowed to enter the jobber-wholesaler-retailer chain. Any disease it may have brought in is still there, together with whatever else it may have been exposed to in the quarantine station. Disease

Opposite: *Musk lorikeet. Before purchasing a lory, do some research on the various species and their availability in the pet trade.*

Opposite top and bottom: *Forsten's rainbow lories,* Trichoglossus haematodus forsteni, *53-day-old nestlings.* ***Right:*** *Adult Forsten's rainbow lory.* ***Below:*** *A ten-day-old dusky lory chick,* Pseudeos fuscata.

Ornate lory. When choosing a lory, check the bird for signs of ill health.

is further transmitted on the wholesale and retail levels where groups of birds are kept together. Thus a wild bird, healthy when caught, has at least three good chances of contracting a disease before being purchased by the hobbyist. Aviary-bred birds do not face these hazards; hence, they are generally healthier.

Part of the problem lies in the fact that it is difficult, if not impossible, to determine non-infected birds. It is easy to spot a sick bird once it has contracted a disease and is showing symptoms, but that can take several weeks in some cases.

Obviously, the best procedure is to note the bird in a shop upon his arrival. If it is still there and healthy looking in two to three weeks, it will probably remain so. Of course, in doing that there is always the chance that someone will buy the bird first. It may be comforting to know that at the time of this writing anyway, lories are not very popular and tend to sit around shops for awhile.

Assuming the bird has been there awhile, it is time for a closer look. Upon first entering the shop, check the entire aviary section carefully, not just the parrots. Often situations in a finch cage can tell you much about the care the parrots are receiving. Are the water troughs full and clean or are they stained with droppings? Are the birds well fed?

When satisfied that the birds are in good health, move on to the bird of your choice. A healthy lory will have bright eyes. Dull or lackluster eyes mean trouble, especially when coupled with an unkempt appearance. Like almost any animal, the lory's eyes are often the key to health.

The bird should have no nasal or ocular discharge. Either is a sign of respiratory problems and could mean serious trouble. Respiratory problems are often manifested in a wheezing sound or a "snick" and sometimes even a shaking of the head.

The bird should be eating well. That can sometimes be hard to determine if the lory is kept in a cage with other birds and is never really easy to tell even if the lory is housed alone. A bird off its food is always unhealthy.

External parasites often trouble members of the parrot family and are visible in several ways. A good close examination of the bird is essential. While holding it in the hands, extend the wings and check the area comparable to the armpit in humans. Mites and lice favor that area in birds, but they are also found on other parts of the body, so a check of the entire bird is advised. At the same time, look for denuded spots and signs of feather picking; these are often also indications of external parasites. The legs should be examined for the parasites that cause scaly-leg. When they are present they are not visible, but rather they leave telltale signs, specifically scales on the legs and feet.

If the bird has any inflammation in the non-feathered areas, there is reason for concern. Should any of the above symptoms be present, it is best to pass the bird by and look for another.

Healthy lories are always full-breasted. Birds that are slight or bony in the upper chest region are probably not eating properly and have not done so for some time.

There should be no matted or sticky feathers. If these are found around the vent, it is a sign of diarrhea; this condition, if noted anywhere else, probably indicates vomiting.

If the lory rests on both feet with its head resting on its back and with its feathers fluffed, it is very sick. Healthy lories generally rest on only one leg and never fluff unless they are cold.

Feather condition in lories, unless abnormally poor, is unimportant. Being high-strung, lories often get roughed up in shipping. The next molt will show a beautiful bird. However, lories will often pick their own feathers for dietary reasons. If there is some essential element missing from the diet, lories will turn to other sources for it. Feather eating is just one such example. Lories have also been known to eat gravel or feces in an attempt to round out their diet. Generally, any perverse eating habit suggests an error in food preparation.

A black-capped lory, Lorius lory. *Never purchase a lory that has a thin breast, as this is a sure sign that something is wrong with the bird.*

It must be added at this point

that a bird passing the above criteria can be assumed to be *currently* in good health. That does not mean it will stay that way. The lory still may have been exposed to diseases that may later surface. The waiting period will cover some of this, but there are never any guarantees.

Once the bird has passed the examination and is purchased, it must begin a new process of acclimation. In the case of the breeder-purchased bird, this may be the only such change in its young life. For the wild-caught individual it may be an old routine, as some have experienced acclimation a dozen or more times before coming to the permanent home. Before packing the bird for the trip, find out exactly what the shop or breeder has been feeding it. While it is widely believed that the food formulas presented in this book are the state of the art and

Rainbow lory. The plumage of a healthy lory need not be in perfect shape, but it should show no matted or sticky feathers.

should be used if possible, it may help with acclimation if the hobbyist knows what foods the bird has been receiving. Many shops keep lories on standard parrot seed as a "temporary" measure until they can be moved out. Regardless of how poor the diet has been, a healthy lory will always eat the nectar presented, as they will try anything sweet and liquid.

The best way to move a bird from shop to home is in the standard cardboard boxes most shops have available for the purpose. While it may seem easier on the bird to move it in the larger cage, lories respond strongly to environmental stimuli and are better off when they cannot see what is going on around them. If a cage must be used for the transportation, it should be covered so the bird cannot see out.

Black lory, Chalcopsitta atra. *This species inhabits western New Guinea and adjacent islands.*

A pair of Swainson's rainbow lories. Due to space restrictions, many pet shops and breeders house two or more lories together.

Once the bird has reached the new home, it should be put immediately into the waiting cage or aviary, preferably alone. Feeding is not necessary until the bird has had a chance to calm down. There has been a lot of change in its life recently and that is not always easy for the bird to deal with. For a tropical bird that has always had consistency in everything in life, from weather to housing, it is a particularly traumatic time.

If necessary, the bird can be placed with another bird if they are to be permanent cagemates. But care must be taken with pet shop birds that are to be released into an aviary. Imported birds often have their wings clipped.

Once the bird has been installed and the food has been offered, it is best to ignore it for a few days except for feeding. It will have enough new things to learn without having to worry about the strange creatures standing with their noses against the cage wall.

Opposite: *Ornate lory testing out its wings.* ***Right:*** *A pair of cardinal lories,* Chalcopsitta cardinalis.

When thinking about adding any bird to the family, the care and feeding should be of primary concern. In the case of lories, this is doubly important. As we said before, lories are unusual birds. Their feeding habits make for all sorts of problems. Fortunately, all problems are remediable with a little work.

Because of their liquid diet, lories are messy birds. It is estimated that their droppings are as much as 99% liquid, further adding to the problem. They can be quite noisy at times, letting out a shrill screech. Some, commonly called screamers, make a habit of this loud display and often drive housemates crazy.

The droppings plus the noise make lories prime candidates for an outside location, preferably far away from quiet-loving avian neighbors. In fact, it would be far better for lories to be kept without neighbors at all since they have a natural compulsion to fight. While keeping lories separately may be inconvenient, it is a lot more convenient than not having the birds at all, which could easily become the situation.

That is not to say that two or more lories cannot live peaceably in the same cage; they can and often do, but keeping them in such arrangements involves a certain amount of risk that the owner should weigh. It is never a good idea to put lories in with other birds. Lories do leave some individual birds unmolested, but in general no bird is safe forever.

While worrying about the welfare of the residents of the aviary, the lory owner should never forget about his own safety. Lories can bite, and hard. It is not unheard of to have a finger fractured by the beak of an irate bird. A little common sense will go a long way in prevention. Whenever a lory must be handled, it should be held in a towel folded into several thicknesses. While this may not prevent the bite, it will certainly lessen its severity. General care in keeping fingers out of striking distance will also help.

In spite of the problems with lories, there are still those who will keep them indoors as house pets. Fortunately, advances in many areas have made this a viable possibility today.

The first step is the choice of the cage. Lories are climbers, so a good parrot cage is in order. Not only must it be able to keep the bird in, but it should also keep predators out. This is a particular problem with cats. Most cats are fascinated with birds and sooner

Opposite: *Yellow-streaked lory,* Chalcopsitta sintillata. *This species, from New Guinea and the Aru Islands, inhabits low-lying savannahs and the forests adjacent to them.*

or later find a way to "play" with the new housemate, much to the bird's—and the owner's—chagrin. Cat-proofing a bird area is always difficult, if not impossible. It is far better to not have the cat in the first place, but that, too, is a matter of choice.

The cat problem can be looked at from a broader perspective. The bird needs to be protected from upsetting environmental stimuli. While this is not possible in an absolute sense, precautions should be taken to lessen such disturbances as much as possible. This is especially critical in the beginning when the bird is trying to acclimate to the new surroundings.

One common upsetting stimulus is the sudden burst of light in a dark room. Lories, like most other animals, are designed to function when darkness goes to light very gradually. The sudden turning on of a light in a dark house is particularly unsettling to birds. Light can be a problem from yet another standpoint. Lories are used to dawn-to-dusk light. Humans have a tendency to sleep past dawn and stay up long after sunset. While it is often assumed by the owner that the bird gets the same eight hours of sleep as does the owner, such is not the case. In the average home, light is present for up to 18 hours a day. This type of situation can disrupt the entire photoperiod of the lory, causing any number of problems. The solution, of course, is to cover the cage at night. Covers should be heavy enough to shield the bird from light yet permit air circulation. Should a light bulb be turned on in the dark room, the cover will also prevent most fits caused by fright.

Barking dogs can also be an upsetting environmental stimulus. This is especially true of a dog that goes from sleep, or at least quiet, to a full-blown manic attack at the first sign of a person or some other dog. If such is the case in the home, the prospective owner must be ready to face the possible consequences.

Cages for medium-sized lories should be fairly large, at least three feet in length. In addition, glass or some other easily cleaned substance should enclose the bottom third of the cage. In that way the droppings are reasonably certain of landing in the cage and not on the floor.

One recent advance in another field has greatly improved the situation of having a lory in the house. For years lory owners have had to put up with a terrible smell that did not seem to fade even when the cage bottom was changed daily. Something has finally been found to help keep the odor under control. The introduction of chlorophyll and other deodorized kitty litters has been a boon to lory households. The litters seem to do an effective job of keeping the odor under control, although daily changing of

Red lory, Eos bornea. *Housing lories in planted aviaries can be self-defeating, as these birds are notoriously destructive when it comes to vegetation.*

the paper is still recommended. If possible, the litter should be spread especially heavily in commonly soiled areas, such as under a perch.

Like any birds, lories will stay healthier if they are kept in relatively clean quarters. Daily changes of the bottom material is only a small part of the task. The glass around the sides should be cleaned whenever it becomes soiled. Cage wires and other surfaces can be cleaned with soap and a scrub brush, preferably on a weekly basis. The same holds true for food or water troughs, although they should be cleaned more often.

Since most lories are kept in parrot cages, they seem to share a common trick. Because the food is mainly nectar, hobbyists often remove the food dishes from the cage before placing the bird inside. This procedure is not recommended for two reasons. The lory diet should include a fruit mix that should be served in a food bowl. Failure to provide this supplement will harm the birds' chances for good health. But probably more frustrating is the fact that lories are great escape artists. These colorful Houdinis are often found walking around outside their cages. The logical assumption on the part of the owner is that the bird has found a way to jimmy the lock on the cage door, so the door gets modified. When the bird is found outside

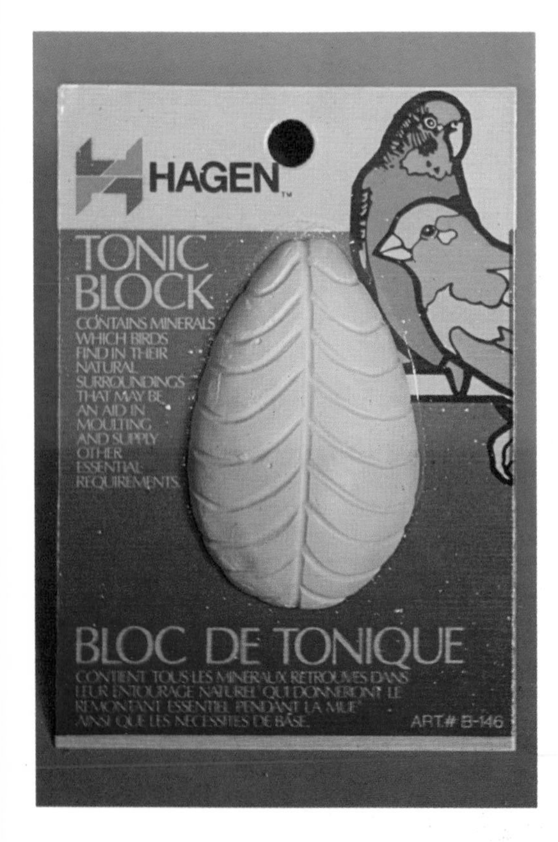

Various types of mineral blocks are available at pet shops.

An assortment of Nylabird® products are available at pet shops. These cage furnishings are made of safe nylon.

again, more modifications follow. Soon the lock is no longer easy for the owner to open and the lory is still strolling around outside the cage. What is actually happening is that this apparently large bird is finding a way to squeeze through that apparently small hole which was left open when the food trough was removed. The tamer the bird, the more likely the escape. While most lories do not go far on these excursions, they can produce quite a mess in the process.

Should there be more than one lory in the cage, the problems are compounded. Invariably one bird can figure out the escape trick and the other cannot. When the owner puts the marauding bandit back into his cage, a fight immediately ensues. Keeping the food dish in place is so much less bothersome.

For the most part, lories are better suited to life in an outdoor aviary than they are to cages. However, with a little more daily maintenance, they can be kept indoors.

The smart hobbyist will, from the beginning, make a place for his lory outdoors. The flight space can be much larger and sanitation is less of a bother. In general, all birds do better outdoors. In the case of lories, most people believe that is the only way to keep them—and they may have a point.

There are two common approaches to aviary building. One is where a concrete floor is used. This is nice from the standpoint of keeping most birds since the concrete can simply be hosed off regularly for sanitation purposes. However, the lories' situation is different. They need some type of soft matter on the bottom of the runs. Most breeders who use concrete floors throw some type of bedding product like peat moss or wood shavings on the floor. This, however, virtually eliminates cleaning convenience and adds the expense of the bedding to an already expensive hobby.

The other school of thought recommends the use of dirt floors which can biologically process the major share of the droppings, lessening the cleaning chores considerably. Dirt floors are easily penetrated by rodents, however, and as rodents can become a major problem in the outdoor aviary, that must be considered. If a dirt floor is used, it is likely that a deeply sunk shield under the walls will prevent any such problems.

The design of the outdoor aviary is simply a matter of common sense. Birds fly upward when alarmed. It can be assumed that a human entering the run will alarm its inhabitants. Therefore, the door should never reach all the way to the top of the cage. A bird flying over the head of its keeper should see only cage wall above. If it

If you plan to keep your lory in an indoor cage, be sure to purchase a cage cover. Many different types are available at pet shops.

sees the door at flight level, it is out.

The most common cage construction is a two-by-four frame covered with a one-inch welded mesh wire that has been galvanized after construction. The caging should then be painted flat black so as not to interfere with the viewing of the birds. An enclosed shelter is not necessary in temperate climates or for summer use; however, it is a good idea. Since lories are cold-hardy, all but the small fairy lorikeet can be kept outdoors year-round in most parts of the country if they are given a good shelter house. The catch is that these birds need to first be put out during the warm months so that they can gradually acclimate to the cold.

A lory cage should be at least three feet in length and should have vertical wires that are close together. In addition, the bottom third of the cage should be covered with plastic, glass, or some other easily cleaned material. The protective material on the cage shown here does not go high enough.

Although some lories may be able to cohabitate, most cannot and should be housed separately.

If, instead, the lories are to be put out only for the warmer months, they should be put out in April and brought back inside in September. Of course, weather in any given year or location can alter those target dates and should be taken into consideration.

Lory cages should always have nesting boxes available year-round, even if there is not a mated pair in the run. Most lories like to use the boxes as perches and will roost in them quite often. The boxes do not necessarily need to be placed within the shelter, but such a location seems to be beneficial to the birds.

If there are to be two or more adjoining avairies, lories will require special treatment. Regardless of what their bird neighbors are, lories have a nasty habit of reaching into the next cage and grabbing anything that moves. This is easily remedied, although the moderate expense has caused many owners to bypass the precaution. The end

result is usually a much greater cost in lost birds. The partitions between cages should be double-wired, with a mesh on each side of the two-by-fours framing the structure. This is usually enough to keep the lories on their own side of the fence and protects all concerned. It is a small price to pay for the safety feature involved.

The lory in the outdoor aviary is no less an escape artist than his indoor counterpart, except that outdoors there is a much greater chance of loss. Thus it is all the more important to ensure that all holes are regularly repaired. A common method of escape is again through the food slots. Rosemary Low suggests a lory-proof feeding station for outdoor aviaries in her book *Lories and Lorikeets* (T.F.H.) that would be of some interest to the hobbyist who intends to keep several cages of lories.

Another way into the larger aviary complex is via a service corridor. This is a small hallway between the lines of pens on the left and right. The keeper enters the corridor, closing the door behind him. In that way the entire complex is sealed before any individual cage is open. If a bird does escape, he can go only into the corridor, where he can be easily netted and returned to the proper cage. Such escapes are more common with the tamer birds. When the food is placed in the cage, less friendly individuals tend to scatter until after the intruder departs.

Many breeders feel that electricity installed in the aviary complex is convenient, and they often wire the individual pens. The temptation then is to provide heat for the shelter houses in the winter. In the case of lories, there is a better use for this modern convenience. If lories have a particular problem during winter, it is the shortage of food. They are browsers and eat all day long.

Opposite: *Blue-crowned lory. Whether you plan to keep your lory indoors or build an outdoor aviary, be sure there are adequate perches.* ***Right:*** *A pair of collared lories,* Phigys solitarius.

How much they eat seems to depend on the length of the day. Winter is hardly the best time for lories to begin eating less, but that is exactly what happens. As the days start to get shorter, the birds settle for less food. Lights added to the aviary and dimmer-controlled to provide 12 hours of feeding time will produce a result as good as heating the shelter and will do it for a lot less money.

There is one common problem with lories in aviaries that the hobbyist should anticipate. They are virtually impossible to capture in a net when they are standing on the mesh. Not that they cannot be netted; that part is simple. The problem is that they will not let go of the mesh. Trying to force the feet off the cage will result in a nasty bite, at best. It is recommended that lories be allowed to land on the floor of a pen before being covered with a net. In this way the chances of getting the bird into the net are greatly increased.

Sooner or later, the keepers of such beautiful birds will begin to think about keeping them in beautiful surroundings. This is a nice thought, but it is not always practical. Because of their feeding habits, lories have a reputation for destroying any plant life available. That reputation is partly justified. Many lories, particularly the larger species, will devour or otherwise destroy plants when available. However, most of the small lories can be kept quite successfully in planted aviaries. If the proper balance of birds and plant life is maintained, it can result in a delightful environment and should be considered a viable possibility.

To date, experts still disagree on whether or not lories need drinking water. As the question is not likely to be answered in the near future, it is best that such water be provided. One thing that is known definitely is that lories like bathing. They should always be provided with knee-deep bathing water for use at their discretion.

In maintaining healthy lories, prevention is the key to success. Much disease is spread and nurtured through carelessness on the part of a bird's owner. Regular disinfecting of all surfaces with which a bird comes in contact goes a long way toward thwarting any disease before it becomes established. Food and water bowls should be soaked in a solution of 4 oz. of liquid laundry bleach to a gallon of water. This process should be done weekly, especially for birds kept in small cages. At least once a month, the cage itself should be either soaked or sprayed with the same solution. Heavily soiled areas can be cleaned with a scrub brush.

For outdoor aviaries, twice a year the caging, supports and all other components should be sprayed down with the same solution in a garden sprayer. Many

The chattering lory is known for the strange gurgling sounds it makes while eating.

large-scale breeders will practice this spraying more often, concentrating on the lower third of the cage only. At any rate, this disinfectant treatment can be one of the best preventives an aviculturist will ever use. Just be sure to remove the birds from the enclosure before the spraying begins.

Aviaries should never be sprayed with any toxic biocides meant for either plant or insect pests. These affect birds adversely.

Like any other birds, lories can be maintained by the home hobbyist. The care is a little more demanding, but the rewards more than make up for it.

Feeding The Lories

Looking at early records of lories in captivity, it is hard to understand how any of them survived at all. There are reports of lories having lived for years on some of the most atrocious food concoctions imaginable. There are even cases in the literature where attempts were made to keep lories on a seed-eater diet. While there was an occasional reported success, proper lory care did not become widespread until efficient nectar formulas were developed and the corresponding successes were noted. Nevertheless, the search for a better food mix still goes on today. While there are the usual state-of-the-art formulas, the research goes on and we can assume that the currently accepted ideal formulas will change many times in the years to come. For now, places like Busch Gardens and the Brookfield and San Diego Zoos are the leaders in food research.

One of the first really successful mixes consisted of Mellen's food, honey, water and canned milk. There was later evidence that milk causes gastro-intestinal problems in lories. That mix was then replaced by brown sugar, water and vitamins.

Recently it became apparent to researchers that lories do not live by nectar alone. In the wild, a lory taking nectar from a flower will also pick up pollen. The papillose tongue takes the pollen and presses it into a form suitable for swallowing. In addition, lories in the wild consume a good deal of fresh fruit and green food.

As more and more was learned about the habits of lories in their natural habitat, the diets offered became better and better, until today it is no longer difficult to maintain lories in a state healthy enough to allow prolific breeding. Unfortunately, while the food has improved the feeding procedure has not become easier. The prospective lory owner should be prepared to make two separate feedings of different nectars, a fruit mix feeding and occasional flower head and green food feedings daily. This is not an easy task, but it is a necessary one if the project of keeping a healthy lory is to be successful.

Brookfield Zoo, outside of Chicago, makes two separate nectars for their lories. Bird Curator Glen Bushor says the same recipe is used by the San Diego Zoo. It is commonly accepted as the best food to date for lories. Recipes follow.

Opposite: *Perfect lorikeet. Feeding a lory the proper diet is, of course, a most important part of the hobby, yet for many years captive lories had to survive on the wrong types of food. Thanks to much time and research, proper formulas are now well known and continue to be improved upon.*

Morning Nectar Mix

1 cup sugar
1 small pinch Fanthaxathin (available from Roche Labs)
4 cups water
3 tablespoons Gevral Protein
2 tablespoons Soyagen (a beverage mix sold in health food stores)
12 cc ABDEC (vitamin drops)
1 teaspoon calcium

Mix all the above in a blender until homogenized. It can be stored up to 48 hours in a covered container kept in a refrigerator. This is meant as a morning feeding and should be given as early as possible in the day. It will be the nectar that is used by the birds through most of the day.

A group of lories at feeding time. It goes without saying that all feed dishes and water containers must be kept scrupulously clean.

Chattering lories in an outdoor aviary. Although it may be easier to forget to remove leftover rations from an outdoor aviary than from a cage kept indoors, it is imperative that all uneaten food be left out for no longer than 48 hours. Some food mixtures may spoil even more quickly.

Evening Nectar Mix
1 cup sugar
3 cups water
12 cc ABDEC (vitamin drops)

Blend as the morning mix. Obviously this is a much simpler formula and is designed for evening and night browsing only.

Lories also need a daily serving of a solid fruit mix. Brookfield Zoo occasionally varies this recipe to include fruits in season. This is the general formula.

Fruit Mix

8 apples
4 pears
1 banana
3 tomatoes
1 papaya
3 cups grapes

These ingredients should be cut up and then thoroughly mixed. Once that is complete, add

½ cup blueberries
½ cup soaked currants
1 cup insectivore diet (prepared food mix)

Again, thoroughly mix and serve in a pan or other broad shallow container.

All of the recipes given make substantial amounts. Obviously, a hobbyist with only one bird will not need to make as large a batch, especially since the nectar lasts only 48 hours. The fruit mix should be offered early, after the morning nectar has been put out.

It is particularly important that lories receive the proper vitamins. Lories require a set of vitamins different from those required by humans, so the standard types bought from health food stores are not adequate. Humans use vitamin D_2, which is totally useless to a lory; instead, D_3 is needed. Birds also need a good deal of vitamin E. The ABDEC mixture will provide all the necessary nutrients.

Many lory experts recommend

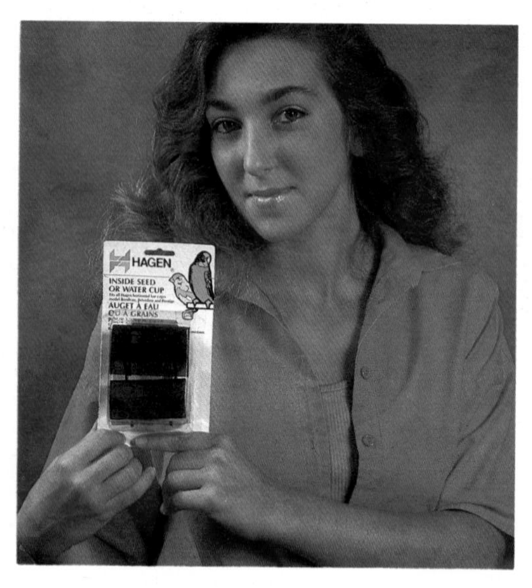

Left: *Many types of feed and water dishes are available at pet shops.* ***Opposite:*** *A pair of red lories on a nest log that has fruit attached to it.*

the use of vitamins in the drinking water. If it should be proved that lories do indeed partake of water, then that may be a good procedure. If, however, it is proved that the entire liquid intake of a lory is in the nectar, such an effort would be wasteful. It is up to the individual to make the decision.

One of the early lory diets consisted of straight seed. While it is known that there is no way such a diet will be beneficial to the birds, there is still the question of whether seeds should ever be fed. Like so many aspects of lory care, there are two points of view. Some experts claim that seed supplements are good for the birds. Brookfield Zoo's Glen Bushor feels that this is a major mistake in the care of lories. Unlike other members of the parrot family, lories lack the strongly muscular gizzard necessary to digest seeds. There are those who believe that ingesting seeds can actually kill a lory. At the same time, there are those who recommend canary seed or spray millet.

Like that of most species, the wild diet of Goldie's lorikeet consists of pollen, nectar, fruit, and berries.

Keeping food fresh can be a problem in warm weather as the nectar mixtures commonly used all tend to spoil in hot temperatures. That makes the twice-daily nectar feeding all the more important.

There are a few cases where the foregoing recipes may not be appropriate. If a bird is acquired unexpectedly, it can take some time to round up all the ingredients necessary to make the mix. In such cases, sugar or syrup dissolved in water will do for a time, but still better would be the liquid from canned fruit, provided it is of the sugar-added variety.

Another special case is that of the newly imported bird. The nectar solutions commonly used in the hobby seem to be too strong

Black-capped lory and chattering lory. Lories differ from other parrots in that they lack the muscular gizzard necessary for digesting seeds.

for the delicately balanced digestive system of the fresh-caught bird. In such cases, the nectar mixture should be diluted with water.

Occasionally one finds a lory that is not interested in the fruit mix offered. Often it is just the way in which it is presented that bothers the bird. Try placing the fruits on top of the aviary or cage (whole fruit or chunks of fruit, not fruit mix). Since lories are basically arboreal creatures, fruit placed overhead is often a sufficient stimulus.

By now, the novice is probably thinking in terms of dollar signs, especially where the fruit mix is concerned. While it can be expensive, it does not have to be. In fact, it can be the cheapest part of owning a lory. Most supermarkets have a good deal of fruit waste daily. Getting a supply of it can be rather simple, as generally one can find a produce manager willing to set aside the

Black-capped lory. Giving a lory a nutritious treat is a wonderful way to supplement the bird's regular diet.

Yellow-streaked lory. This species is known for extracting nectar from ripening tree stalks.

culls for daily pickup. This procedure is especially helpful for those persons raising many lories.

Occasional treats are not only welcomed by the birds but can also go a long way toward improving their health. All flowerheads that are normally discarded should, instead, be recycled through a lory. This includes dandelions, spent annuals and any other type of flower available. The only problem here is that the hobbyist must be certain that the flowers have never been sprayed with a biocide of any type. Birds are particularly susceptible to the common biocides and should never have such exposure.

Mealworms, fed when available, will be relished wholeheartedly and will also add to the quality of the diet.

Feeding lories is not easy. There is a great deal of time and effort that goes into the preparation of any food. In the cases of lories, most owners feel the effort pays great dividends.

Breeding Lories

With birds, as with most other animals, the ultimate goal of the hobby is procreation. There are those who feel that each hobbyist should ultimately aim toward a breeding program for his birds. While it is a fact that there are those who want just one bird for home enjoyment, nevertheless breeding is important to a good many hobbyists and must be considered in any text on the subject.

Breeding lories is no tougher than breeding other members of the parrot family, and in some cases it is easier. If the hobbyist has gone to all the trouble of providing a good diet, he will find that, by comparison, breeding these birds is a snap.

In the wild the larger species of lories nest in hollow tree trunks and the smaller species such as the Swainson's nest in hollow branches. Breeding usually commences at two to three years of age.

In captivity it is the job of the breeder to provide the bird with those necessities that are not available due to confinement in a cage or aviary. A good start is to find a hollow trunk or branch and fill it with a **few** bark chips or shavings—and I emphasize the word **few**. Brookfield Zoo has in the past suffered losses because the eggs were irretrievably buried. This is especially true in the case of shavings. But lories are not picky birds. A square nesting box or even a small wicker basket will be accepted readily.

Whether using tree parts or wooden boxes, be sure to use a heavy wood like oak or poplar with openings suitable for the size bird it is to accommodate. Another type of nesting enclosure is the small metal drum commonly used for waterfowl nest boxes. In any case, pine and other soft woods are not advisable as the lories will quickly destroy the accommodations with their exuberant chewing habits.

Once the nesting boxes are put in position, they should stay there year-round. Not only do lories breed all year, but commonly the boxes are used as perches. Often the most loved perch in the pen is the nesting box.

It has been reported that lories have no more than two chicks per litter with the exception of *Glossopsitta* species, which generally lay three to four eggs. However, noted observers in this field have reported the number per clutch to be three to six. In this still-new science there is still a lot to be learned.

***Opposite:** Although some experts consider the breeding of lories to be easier than breeding other parrots, lories are just as difficult to sex as many other parrot groups.*

Opposite, top left: *Iris lorikeets,* Trichoglossus iris. **Opposite, top right:** *Duyvenbode's lory,* Chalcopsitta duivenbodi. **Opposite bottom:** *The black lory, shown here, and Duyvenbode's lory are among the largest lory species.* **Above:** *A black lory chick raised in the San Diego Zoo.*

Once the aviary is made ready, it is time to introduce the birds. This is where many breeding schemes go awry. It sounds simplistic, but the most important thing in breeding is to get a pair. This is especially tough with lories since both sexes are generally identical in appearance. The best way to establish breeding pairs for lories, or for any other bird for that matter, is to let them pair off on their own. Lories have a strong desire to pick their own mates. Once they pair off, they tend to stay together, so the time spent in letting them choose for themselves is time well spent.

Ideally, pairs are purchased from a breeder. When the birds are old enough to start breeding, six or seven are put into one large pen with each bird wearing a differently colored leg band. The birds are then given a few days to do any pairing. Generally lories are pretty quick to mate and will begin nesting immediately. The breeder then notes the band colors of the birds that are busy with housekeeping. Later they can be netted and moved to a pen of their own where the breeding process will continue, it is hoped, for years to come. It is at this point that the birds should be purchased. Of course, this is the ideal situation. While it may occur regularly with the more common birds, in the case of lories the opportunity will seldom present itself.

More likely a group of six or seven lories will be available. The prospective owner will have to guess as to the sexes. Even if luck is on the hobbyist's side and the two birds chosen are of the opposite sex, it still does not mean that they will ever mate. In fact, in some cases fighting will occur that can culminate in the death of one of the birds. For that reason, the birds must be watched closely for signs of conflict.

In her book *Lories and Lorikeets*, Rosemary Low contends that a good way of getting two birds of the opposite sex is to look at a group of the same species. Then, by selecting the one with the largest beak and head and the one with the smallest beak and head, the hobbyist can greatly improve his chances of obtaining two sexes. While it is of little help in choosing the pair, once a pair is established the male can be seen to generally have a broader upper mandible than the female.

When a breeding pair is established, the birds quickly go about the business of making little birds. The eggs are laid on alternate days in most cases, and the female spends most of her time with them from this point on. The incubation period is 22-28 days depending on the species and the individuals involved. The male now spends a good deal of his time on the nest with the female. It is generally believed,

A pair of 36-day-old chattering lories. Young chattering lories have brownish bills and dark brown irises, while adults have orange bills and yellowish brown irises.

however, that he is keeping her company and is not actively participating in the incubation process. During this period and throughout the rearing stages, the nest remains spotless. Lories are excellent housekeepers, and when they finally leave the nest it will still look unused.

One aspect of the breeding

Above: *Fairy lorikeets,* Charmosyna pulchella. *In this species the females are distinguished by the yellow patches on the sides of the rump.* **Opposite:** *Yellow-streaked lory in foreground; dusky lory in background.*

process is particularly annoying to human neighbors. The female carries on what seems like a continuous squawking during the period of incubation. In response to this nagging, the male feeds her. It is hard to imagine that one bird can eat so much, but the squawking goes on. Three to four weeks later, the new lories, barely down-covered, emerge from the eggs. At this point the second part of the breeding process begins.

Fortunately, the rearing part of the breeding process is a snap from the owner's standpoint. The parents take care of everything. It is not necessary even to provide a rearing food since the nectar recipes in this book are so rich. It has been reported, though, that mealworms (if available) should be offered during this time.

In two to three months, the young will be weaned. It is highly desirable for them to be removed from the parents before the latter begin to show signs of nesting again. If at that time the young are not removed, they will be looked upon as intruders and will be treated as such. In general, this occurs the following spring, but it may occur at just about any time.

Because of the high price the birds bring, breeding lories is becoming big business. The average breeder seeks ways of increasing his production as economically as possible. One of the best ways is "fostering," the care and nurturing of eggs and

A pair of lories may or may not be compatible mates.

chicks by some other less expensive bird. This process entails taking newly laid eggs from the nest and putting them into the nest of another bird that also has a clutch of eggs. The older eggs can remain with the parents or be discarded at the breeder's discretion. This is not a common procedure with lories, but it is possible. Fostering is far more common with birds such as doves and pigeons.

Another possibility is hand-rearing. In this instance, the eggs can be kept in an incubator until they hatch and then the young are hand-fed by the breeder. While a slightly more prevalent practice than fostering, this takes a tremendous amount of time and effort. The main purpose of fostering or hand-rearing is the possible increase in numbers produced. Once the eggs are taken from the nest, the parents will usually begin the breeding process over again, producing another clutch in two to three weeks.

While either process is highly technical in nature, each can be successfully completed by the hobbyist. Those interested in hand-rearing should check the detailed description contained in *Lories and Lorikeets.*

Once the hobbyist has entered the world of breeding, almost nothing else will do. Both spiritually and financially, the rewards of producing the birds are habit forming. That habit tends to last a lifetime.

A pair of rainbow lories standing on a nest log. Lories enjoy perching on nesting boxes that have been hung from the ceiling.

***Left:** Red-flanked lorikeets,* Charmosyna placentis. ***Bottom left:** Papaun lorikeets,* Charmosyna papou. *Birds of the genus* Charmosyna *are known for their small size.* ***Bottom right:** Cardinal lories.* ***Opposite:** Red lory.*

Diseases and Veterinary Care

Any time we take an animal into our family, it implies a certain acceptance of responsibility. Like children, animals need constant care, if only a regular check-up to determine the current state of health and happiness. But the responsibilities go further. There is always the possibility that any bird will become ill or injured. When that happens, it is often too late to be doing the seemingly trivial things that could have easily been done beforehand. For that reason, the things that can be done in advance should be done. Of prime importance is finding a qualified veterinarian.

In the last few years the bird hobby has snowballed. Because of the crowding in our cities and the smallness of our living spaces, birds are becoming increasingly popular as house pets. Walking a dog in downtown Chicago, New York or Los Angeles is too much commitment for the average person. A bird is the perfect answer. As a result, the hobby is booming.

Unfortunately, changes in the veterinary field occur more slowly than those in the pet business. Partly because of the years required to enter the field and partly because of the uncertain (as some see it) future of the bird hobby, veterinary schools are not graduating many bird specialists. It is more usual for a vet to specialize in cows and horses or dogs and cats. Nevertheless, there are some veterinarians around who are well versed in avian medicine. Some of them are known nationally for their work. However, those with such experience are few indeed. That makes them hard to find—a problem the panicking hobbyist does not need at three in the morning when his bird becomes sick.

Before the bird is brought home or immediately thereafter, the hobbyist should find a veterinarian versed in bird matters. It may take several phone calls, but generally in any area there is someone who will fill the bill. Often inquiring at local pet shops will produce the desired information. Once the doctor is chosen, he should be contacted about adding your name to his patient list. It might not be a bad idea to have the new arrival vet-checked immediately to determine its health and to get to know the veterinarian. That is a most important aspect of bird health.

In the wild, lories are very hardy birds; they are not susceptible to most diseases and are vigorous inhabitants of their regions. They are long-lived and carry longevity

Opposite: *A musk lorikeet. Note the clear eyes and bright, clean plumage on this bird.*

Lories of the genus Eos *are large birds with extensive red plumage.* ***Above:*** *Violet-necked lory,* Eos squamata. ***Opposite, top left:*** *Buru red lory,* Eos bornea cyanonothus. ***Opposite, top right:*** *Blue-streaked lory,* Eos reticulata. ***Opposite, bottom left:*** *Gueby violet-necked lory,* Eos squamata guenbyensis. ***Opposite, bottom right:*** *Black-winged lory,* Eos cyanogenia.

into captivity if provided with adequate nutrition, care, diet and temperature.

Unfortunately, the importation process causes all types of problems. Wholesalers bring in huge quantities of parrots. Many more are smuggled in illegally. In general, these birds are then kept togther in massive, overcrowded conditions. Under such stresses, it takes only one sick bird to begin an epidemic. Disease spreads fast when resistance is low. Add to that the problem caused by the sheer trauma of captivity, and you have a bird in a very precarious situation. For that reason, more lories are sick in their first weeks of ownership than in all other time periods put together. Once the bird has made it through a few months in the home, there will probably be no problems other than the aging process.

As with any animal, including the human variety, prevention is always the best policy. If better sanitation were used by importers and quarantine stations, there would probably be less reason for the concern bird owners have about adding new birds to the aviary, especially if the birds are given an adequate diet. By practicing such fundamental precautions, you can see how easy it really could be to keep the birds healthy.

Nevertheless, the hobbyist has to take a chance on the new bird. Once the preliminary period is over though, there is no reason at all for taking risks. Clean cages and bacterial-control spray are generally sufficient, when coupled with a good diet, to prevent most common ailments. Of course, nothing can be done for degenerative diseases, but for most lory owners that is years down the road.

Since home birds do not usually come in contact with other birds, the hobbyist need not be as concerned about transmissible diseases as are pet shops or wholesalers. If the cage is cleaned every few days, the bird is properly fed and clean water is available, the hobbyist is doing the job adequately and it will show in the health of the bird.

Should all the appropriate precautions be taken, that still does not relieve the owner of the responsibility of regularly checking the bird's health. Such checks consist simply of examining the bird as it sits in the cage and up close while holding it in the hands. The superficial check, looking at the bird in the cage, should be done daily. It takes less than a minute to check all the pertinent points, and most problems can be spotted early, before they become dangerous to the bird. The hand check should be done at least once monthly and should include a close examination of the bird.

Like any animal, the health check in lories is simply a matter of looking for symptoms. When

A pair of rainbow lories. When it comes to the health care of lories, prevention is the key word.

the bird is in the cage, look for any of the following:

1. Listlessness;
2. Lessening of eating or drinking;
3. Ocular or nasal discharge;
4. Diarrhea;
5. Denuding or ruffling of feathers;
6. Rough or scaley legs.

In the case of diarrhea, it takes some practice at spotting a problem since the droppings of the lory are always 99% liquid. The best way of spotting the problem is to check the vent area. That will be done in the handheld check. In this check-up, the bird should be examined closely and palpated to check for any number of problems. The following are the most common symptoms:

1. Mites or lice;
2. Badly soiled vent area;
3. Oral discharge.

Any of these could indicate more than one problem. To examine for mites or lice, the feathers must be separated to be able to see the skin. Any "inhabitants" found among the feathers are probably one of the two mentioned groups, but not necessarily. At any rate, a veterinarian should be consulted to identify the pest and prescribe a medication. The most common places for the pests to invade are the skin folds on the legs and under the wings in the area

Above: *A pair of chattering lories. Before placing any plants or branches into the habitat of your lories, be sure they have not been sprayed with chemicals of any kind.* **Opposite:** *A young chattering lory.*

A pair of yellow-and-green lorikeets. If you suspect that one of your birds is sick, quarantine it as soon as possible.

corresponding to the human armpit. While an infested bird will usually show signs in those places, this will not always be so; the entire body of the bird should be checked.

After turning the bird on its back, look at the vent area. A healthy lory produces liquid wastes but is able to propel those wastes over quite a distance. When the bird is suffering from diarrhea, there is frequently "dripping" or it lacks the ability to launch the droppings; either condition leads to a soiled vent region.

The mouth should be checked for any kind of discharge or growth, particularly white fluffy matter and hard dark matter caked around either the inside or the outside of the mouth.

After these checks are completed, the bird should be palpated to determine fullness of breast and to ensure that there are no tumorous growths forming. Either of these signs can indicate problems. If the bird's breast begins to emaciate, there is a serious problem.

Diseases of birds are many, but few are common. In general, once a bird is established in the home, illness is rare. In the isolated instance of the sick bird, it is helpful to have some familiarity with the diseases the veterinarian is referring to. Some of the more common diseases are listed below.

Pacheco's disease is a herpes virus infection that is fairly common among parrots, especially those fresh from quarantine stations and other mass housing arrangements.

Salmonella infection in birds is much like the same problems in humans. This bacterial infection is generally prevented by good hygiene, especially where food and water are concerned.

Chlamydia is transmissible to humans and therefore is of greater concern than many of the other parrot diseases. Such is the case also with *ornithosis* and *psittacosis.* All three are generally treatable by using either chlortetracycline or Aureomycin. This treatment is something that should be done by the wholesalers before the bird is sent to a pet shop so that actual outbreak of the disease can be prevented.

Anemia is always a sign of something lacking in the diet, as is any perverse eating habit. In the case of anemia, vitamin B_{12} in the nectar is a good preventive. Rosemary Low suggests black currant flavored Cytacon for B_{12}.

A rainbow lorikeet. It is wise to make regular health checks on each bird that you keep.

Above and opposite: *Black-capped lories. Perches are necessary for all birds. Using safe natural branches encourages the bird to change its grip frequently, thus exercising the muscles in the feet.*

Candidiasis is a mouth infection caused by the fungus *Candida albicans* that can also spread to air sacs in the body. Once this extent of spread has been reached, the bird cannot be saved. That is why it is imperative to check regularly for oral discharge. The recommended treatment is to avoid the use of antibiotics and to administer massive doses of vitamin A. Reducing the sugar content of the nectar is also suggested.

Like any other warm-blooded animals, lories are also sometimes host to worms, particularly tapeworms. This is one area where the hobbyist can do his own diagnosing and treatment. The common tapeworm medication prescribed for children does the job nicely when added in small quantities to the nectar. Nevertheless, it is best to get exact dosage recommendations from the veterinarian before beginning the feeding of any medication.

Of course, lories also suffer from the common old-age-related degenerative diseases such as glaucoma, tumors, neoplasms and conditions of the heart and circulatory system much like those in humans of advanced age. As is also the case with humans, there is little that can be done for such problems.

At Chicago's Brookfield Zoo, the common Swainson's lories experienced many convulsions that no one was able to explain. The convulsive attacks would last for two or three days and then the birds would apparently recover. The recovery period lasted for not more than a few days, however, when the attacks would occur again. The curators were never able to determine when the convulsions would start again or when they would stop. The problem kept recurring until the birds died. It has been several years since that incident, and the cause has still not been discovered. The incident points out that, because lories are new birds to the hobby, there is much we do not yet know. As their popularity increases and more research is done, this situation should improve.

When a bird is found to be sick, this requires immediate action. We cannot stress enough the importance of prompt veterinary care. Short of that, the hobbyist can do certain things until such help is available. When a bird is found to be ill, it should immediately be isolated in a cage kept at 80°F. Because of the high temperature, the nectar will need to be changed several times daily. The best way to maintain the temperature is by the use of a

Opposite: *A variety of accessories for your lory are available at your local pet shop.*

PENN PLAX
BIRD ACCESSORY CENTER

Universal Seed and Water Cup
Seed Cup with Perch
Egg Treat Cup
Copper Cockatiel Bell
Copper Budgie Bell
Seed Cup with Mirror and Perch
Automatic Twin Feeder/waterer
Jumbo Fountain Feeder
Copper Parrot Bell
PLAY PACK
Small Play Bird
Funnel Seed Feeder
Seed Cup with Mirror and Perch
3" Wooden Bird Swing
Ferris Wheel
Swing with Beads & Bell
Seed or Water Fountain
Perch Swing Bell
Hanging Swing with Bell
Bird Bath with Mirror
Hanging Mirror with Bell
Hanging Mirror
Landing Perch with Mirror and Beads
Seed Feeder
Seed Guard (For Bird Cages)
Universal Clip-on Perches 10"
PLAY PACK
Bird Feeder
Bird Bath

Left: *Emerald lorikeets,* Neopsittacus pullicauda. ***Bottom left:*** *Blue-crowned lory.* ***Bottom right:*** *Collared lory.* ***Opposite:*** *Tahitian lory,* Vini peruviana.

heat lamp. The lamp should be directed so it lights only one part of the cage, thus allowing the bird to escape the heat if necessary.

Once the cage is set up, the bird can be treated with one of the common wide-spectrum antibiotics available in most pet shops. The antibiotic should be placed in the nectar and the resulting mixture fed in small amounts to ensure that all of the antibiotic is taken. If the bird is off its food, the nectar and antibiotic can be force-fed with a teaspoon.

A varied lorikeet. No matter what species of lory you plan to keep, a little common sense will go a long way.

Whenever a disease occurs it is vital that the cages, food and water utensils, and all other objects the bird came in contact with be cleaned and disinfected; the bleach and water solution will do the job well.

Unlike many other animals, lories really need little in the way of routine maintenance. Regular trimming of the claws and maybe an occasional filing of the beak are all they should ever require.

The only way a lory can be beautiful is if it is happy, and happiness in lories is a function of health. That, more than anything else, will determine the enjoyment the hobbyist can derive from the bird.

CONCLUSION

When the reader began this book, he was bombarded with all the bad points of lories. The author's reasoning was that the good features are obvious. By the time the reader has come to this point, the hobbyist knows exactly what he is in for when he adds a lory to the family. If that desire is still present, then perhaps he is the type of person that will do well with a lory. In that endeavor, I wish you well.

Index